With love to Ben and Sinead
on their wedding day - 2nd September 2006
Something for the soul
Wishing you many, many happy years
together
With fond love, Cathy

HAIKU
for LOVERS

HAIKU
for LOVERS

Compiled by Manu Bazzano

MQP

For Sarita, now and always

Thank you
David Scott for being Dave. Amanda Little and Sugra Zaman. Leanne Bryan and
Ljiljana Baird at MQ Publications. To all the haiku poets who help to keep haiku alive in
the 21st Century. And to Sarita Doveton, for reminding me of the Beloved.

Haiku for Lovers Copyright © 2003 MQ Publications Limited

Selection and Introductory text Copyright © 2003 Manu Bazzano

DESIGN: Balley Design Associates

EDITOR: Leanne Bryan

Published by MQ Publications Limited

12 The Ivories, 6–8 Northampton Street, London N1 2HY

Tel: +44 (0)20 7359 2244 / Fax: +44 (0)20 7359 1616

email: mail@mqpublications.com

website: www.mqpublications.com

ISBN: 1-84072-412-9

Printed and bound in China

MQ 10 9 8 7 6 5 4 3 2 1

the weight,
the weight we carry
is love.

ALLEN GINSBERG

LOVE IS, according to the Czech poet Rainer Maria Rilke, the "obscure interval between birth and death." The implication is that precious little else happens in our life which carries the same meaning, the same intensity. Doubtless, we toil and struggle, and busy ourselves with pursuing and acquiring all sort of objects, only to realize, sooner or later, that they do not give us the satisfaction we crave.

Love gives us the golden opportunity to surrender the root cause of our anguish: the self. Without surrendering the self—

even momentarily—neither love nor poetry, and haiku poetry in particular, are possible. For love—ordinary, imperfect, human love—is at its very core a form of generosity, the first of the six "transcendental perfections" expounded by the Buddha. Even noble pursuits such as science and religion are refined stimulants, ways in which the self busies itself, beating around the bush, postponing its own inevitable extinction through love.

We all possess this yearning, deep down, to give ourselves up. We also sense that without having experienced love we are merely killing time. Unless we have fully revealed ourselves to another, unless we have been exposed at some point in our life to the elemental forces of love, we have not truly lived.

And what is Art, after all, if not a sublimation of love? And doesn't religion borrow its ecstasies from the sighs and cries of the lovers' bedroom?

Love is a journey with a beginning, a middle, and an end. It is fashionable nowadays to speak of the journey for the journey's sake, but, as D. H. Lawrence reminds us, we undertake love's journey precisely in order to arrive somewhere. Naturally, most of us get stuck someplace along the journey. We are all very fond of beginnings, and our culture, when it comes to love, is essentially a honeymoon culture. Addiction to the heady wine of romance harbors the disappointments that inevitably follow; we cannot have perennial summer, for that would mean living in a picture postcard.

The lover's glance has stirred up in us much more than we bargained for. If we then undertake the journey until the end, perhaps no other discipline or training is needed.

"When I love thee not, Chaos is come again," exclaims Shakespeare's Othello. When we are not ruled by the gods of love, we are at the mercy of our own ego, and of its unreasonable demands. We then inhabit a world of fear, ignorance, and aggression. We end up with a semi-detached in hell, or with an "apartment in the City of Death" as the mystic poet Kabir has it.

Heightened by love, life appears in its true colors. Meetings and separations are intensely felt, the joys and chagrins of love remove our protective membrane and allow us to perceive life in its raw magnificence.

Lovers gain access to that same source from which artists draw inspiration, from which saints procure their visions. They all realise—albeit for a brief spell—that they are part of the vast ocean of life and death, rather than individual waves with their particular destinies.

With sexual union, we lose our discontinuity and bathe again in the sacred river. Separation is—for a brief moment—gone. The same happens when we practice meditation regularly: We forget the self, as it is said in the Zen tradition, and when the self is forgotten, "the ten thousand things come to the fore."

How to integrate the orgasmic experience into the everyday life of a couple—and how to integrate the realization in the meditation hall into that same everyday life—these are the parallel, strikingly similar tasks that lovers share with spiritual practitioners.

"Haiku for Lovers" might sound at first like a contradiction in terms. Haikus are unadorned and lonely in their appearance whereas love is overflowing and ecstatic. Haikus often deal with heightened states of aloneness, whereas love is a celebration of union. Experience tells us, however, that unless we have savored the joys of solitude, we cannot truly and intimately relate to another. We also sense, in spite of centuries of romantic literature, that intense, complex emotions are best conveyed with economy of words and a terse simplicity. A "haiku moment" occurs when the self is momentarily forgotten, and the wild wind of reality floods our room carrying gifts from the nearby woods. Haiku is a moment of reality expressed in three lines of verse. We rarely perceive reality, for we are either too busy making plans for the future or trying to relive the past through memory. When reality knocks at our door, the world is full of wonder. We become exposed to joy and pain, to an overwhelming sense of mystery. We realise that, deep down, we know nothing, and that this "not knowing" is the most intimate knowledge of all.

Haiku has its spiritual origins in Zen and Taoism. It is the very flowering of Eastern culture. To appreciate haiku is at the same time to honour Taoism, Zen, the tea ceremony, the art of flower arrangement—all the rich and wonderful spiritual traditions of ancient China and Japan. We have also been blessed, since the last century, with some excellent Western haiku, the fruit of a natural process, parallel to the spreading of Zen Buddhism in the West.

There are various aesthetic guidelines in haiku. The first is simplicity. The greatest master of haiku, Matsuo Basho, learned and perfected the basic element of this poetic form; that it is possible to compress in an harmonious way, and within few syllables, meaningful feelings and insights. Or, as Allen Ginsberg has it, maximum communication, minimum number of words.

Other meaningful aesthetic qualities are the avoidance of the sublime and the celebration of the richness of the plain, an acute awareness of the physical, and a refreshing lack of self-centeredness. These are all characteristics that would no doubt benefit all forms of poetry.

The classic poetic dilemma of realism versus the imagination or the present versus eternity is happily dissolved in haiku. Using the imagination in the present is the very essence of the poetic life. Looking at an object intimately is at once precise observation, and awareness of the infinity breathing inside it. For this reason, in haiku we find Classic poetry reconciled to Modern European poetry.

A "haiku moment" occurs when we open our eyes and look. We step into the river of life, and realise that we can't step twice in the same river. Not even once, in fact. The experience is a "small death." We sense the fragility and raw quality of life, its inexplicability. For a brief moment, we forget our illusion of separateness. We are in the river. We are the river.

The haiku world is the raindrop world. The true haiku poet is intensely absorbed in the physical and acutely aware of its transience. Such loving absorption allows her to perceive phenomena with equanimity: Nothing is too high or too low.

This anthology includes some senryu poetry. Most haiku magazines and anthologies in English also publish senryu, a poetic form so similar to haiku that it has become increasingly difficult to set the two apart. Traditionally, Japanese senryu are jocose, anonymous, and proverbial. Nature—a key element in haiku—shifts into the background. What concerns a Japanese or Western senryu is the imperfection of the human condition, the weaknesses and foibles of human beings; our fears, hopes and shortcomings. No wonder so many of them deal with love...

Dividing love's journey into three stages is a way to chart the rise and unfolding of Desire. The world, the saying goes, is in love with itself. From the initial bolt of lightning to the gentle unfolding, to the level of "harmonic love," we become acquainted with the various degrees and tonalities of desire. In the process, we discover and come to terms with the whole range of human feelings and emotions, from the deepest joy to the pain of separation. We lay ourselves bare to the siege of love and beauty. We have known love: Now we can truly call ourselves human.

Love knows no East or West, North or South. It transcends the boundaries of race, culture, and language. Whether experienced by an ancient Chinese poet, a European troubadour, or a contemporary city dweller, love remains as rich and as unfathomable as ever. It testifies to a deep longing, and in some cases, to a deep fulfilment: the latter is a sign that the river has reached the ocean, and that we have found true satisfaction in the arms of the beloved. The old separation between "me" and the world has melted away. The world has regained its natural fluidity.

Manu Bazzano

Honeymoon

1

AFTER THE FIRST MEETING, this ordinary room is transformed into the garden of Eden. Time's gray hand becomes golden: It punctuates the gaps between now and the next rendezvous.

In sexual passion, we inherit the sun, the moon and the stars, and in the languid embrace of afterlove, we are closer to the heart of the universe. Our blood sings in dark veins, and we discover the night.

The long, sleepless hours devoted to sex and love wash us clean, and in the morning we find radiance, lightness in our step, a courage we did not know we possessed. We find a morning sunbeam on the face of our loved one.

We love, and are loved in return. We are the first woman and the first man walking on earth, and today is the only day. We have no history, and thus no regrets. We have no future, and thus we belong to eternity. All other human endeavors seem gray and anaemic when perceived through the honeymoon glow. Logic and reason seem skeletal knick-knacks, rusty tools for mere survival.

Lovers shrug off the gravity of the world with their laughter: their laughter adds music to the world: "She enters / Sunshine, waves and violins…"

Eros, like poetry, is a dancing child in the dull abattoir of law and necessity. Looking at nature through tears of joy, it appears as if broken up in iridescent colors. Lovers access fluidity, the ability to be anyone, to dare anything.

*Watched her approach
and as we finally pass
our umbrellas touch*

Seán O'Connor

through binoculars
    a woman looking at me
through binoculars

MYKEL BOARD

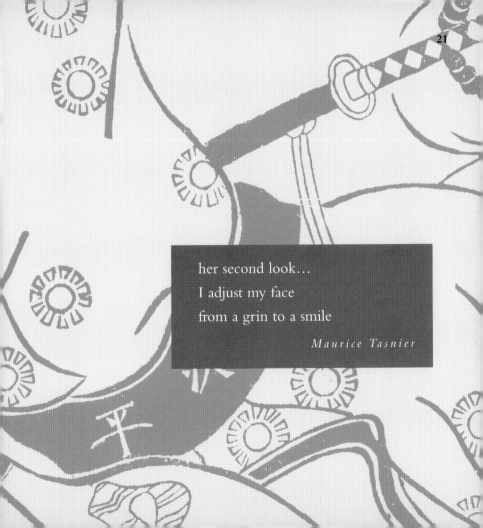

her second look…
I adjust my face
from a grin to a smile

Maurice Tasnier

he looks again—
the girl in the summer dress
has closed her eyes

David Steele

She enters
sunshine, waves and violins
then leaves

Basem Farid

Festival pathos:
falling hopelessly in love
with a lady juggler.

Seishi Yamaguchi /
Tr. Takashi Kodaira and Alfred H. Marks

The lily she held
in her hand as she passed by
left its fragrance here

SEISHI YAMAGUCHI /
TR. TAKASHI KODAIRA AND ALFRED H. MARKS

in her perfumed
wake I walk to class
kicking yellow leaves

John Hazelton

Strolling for miles
arm in my pocket
hoping she'll take it

KEN JONES

waiting for you
one, two, three petals
on the seat

Akiko Sakaguchi

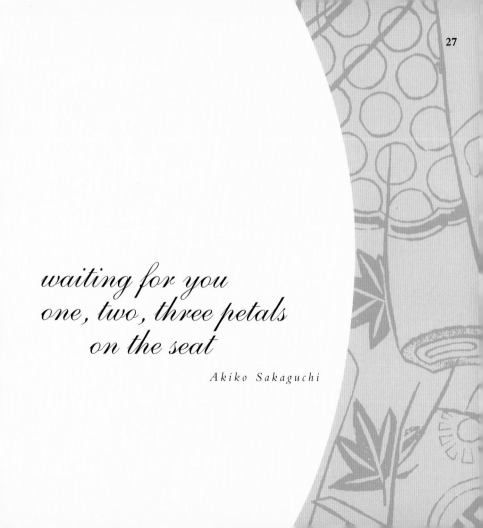

sun shining
through her skirt
and she knows it

Robert Gray

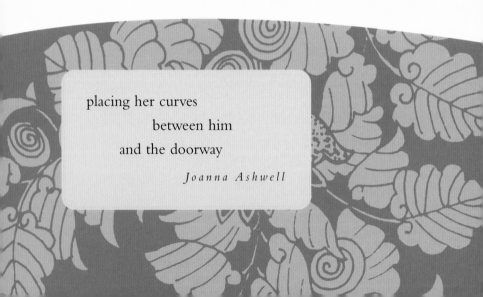

placing her curves
between him
and the doorway

Joanna Ashwell

Leading him in...
my bracelet
jangling.

Alexis Rotella

we talked   while outside
the sky changed from wintry blue
through green to black night

COLIN BLUNDELL

memorable night out
film-plot unknown
still

Douglas M. Henly

*too quick to reply
cutting my tongue
on the envelope*

John Stevenson

Peach trees all in bloom
to make a hair ornament
for the love goddess.

Seishi Yamaguchi /
Tr. Takashi Kodaira and Alfred H. Marks

cemetery

our first feared

kiss

Christopher W. Howell

away from eyes
the stairwell holds
us in its arms

ROD WILLMOT

she can't read
he can't write, yet between them
a romance

Senryu / Tr. Makoto Ueda

Spring rain:
　Clinging to each other
　　Under one umbrella.

Natsume Soseki / Tr. Soiku Shigematsu

tissue paper kisses

melting

in the rain

MAGGIE WEST

all my expectations
my lover letting down
her hair

BRIAN TASKER

She is naked now
and the rose hue of her breast
tints a gift of pearls.

Gilbert Bowen

The white of her neck
as she lifts her hair for me
to undo her dress

Bernard Lionel Einbond

A crane carries
All my burning passion
Through the autumn night.

ISHIDA HAKYO / TR. R. H. BLYTH

that first time in bed—
surprised at how fluent
our body language

Frank Dullaghan

first eye to eye
then hand to hand
and mouth to mouth

Senryu / Tr. Makoto Ueda

moon flowers!
when a woman's skin
is revealed

Kaga no Chiyo /
Tr. Patricia Donegan and Yoshie Ishibashi

how long it seems
when you unwind a woman's sash
while lying in bed!

Senryu / Tr. Makoto Ueda

Stand erect my love;
let the divinity of your eyes
fall upon me.

Sappho / Tr. Kevin Bailey

I will share
This pomegranate with you,
Splitting it at the seam.

Takeo / Tr. R. H. Blyth

afterwards
from the bedroom window
cool moonlight

John Shimmin

kept awake
by the silence
of her breathing

Maurice Tasnier

early morning voices
and the scent of you
half a pillow away

John Barlow

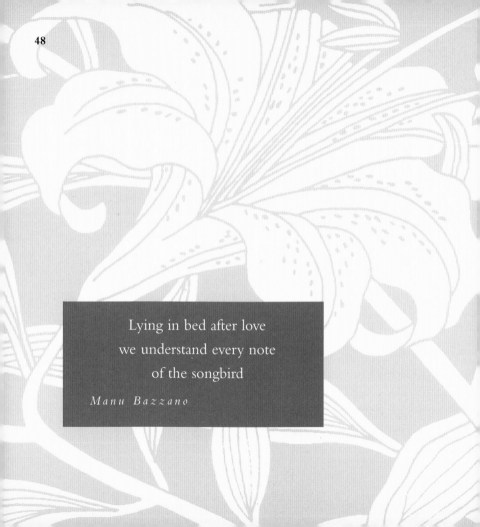

Lying in bed after love
we understand every note
of the songbird

Manu Bazzano

morning shyness—
after our bath
she wraps herself in a towel

Brian Tasker

the thousand colors
in her plain brown hair—
morning sunshine

BERNARD LIONEL EINBOND

You kissed me:
the sun lit up
on my dumbfounded lips.

Claudia Baldini / Tr. Manu Bazzano

Looking for you
through hundreds
of love haiku

Manu Bazzano

Your gaze:
a warm haven
a soft answer

GEMMA CRISCUOLI / TR. MANU BAZZANO

First cold dawn;
Sharing the same knit sweater
  we watch the moon set

Lorraine Ellis Harr

*frozen darkness:
someone knocks
at my heart*

Toshimi Horiuchi

after she's gone
unwinding
a long hair from my sweater

Brian Tasker

Lying—
I tell him I'm not looking
for a prince.

Alexis Rotella

failing to intrude
on our lovemaking
his bagpipe practice

Nick Woodward

Makes the eye happy—
the whiteness
of the lover's fan.

Yosa Buson / Tr. Robert Hass

I'm glad I stuck my
tongue right down your ear although
it tasted waxy.

JENNIFER WALLACE

She removes
her panties
full moon

George Swede

The shrine maiden's hands held over the charcoal pan radiated love.

Seishi Yamaguchi /
Tr. Takashi Kodaira and Alfred H. Marks

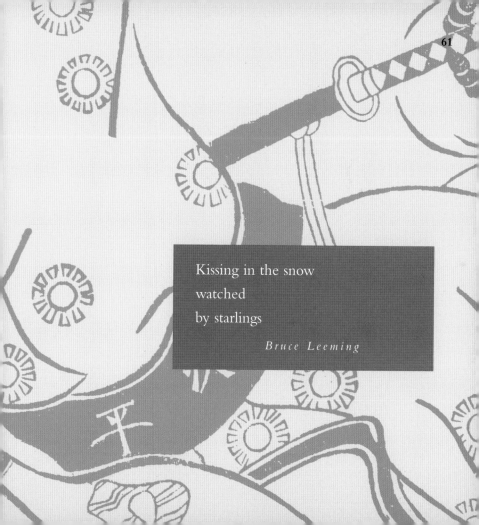

Kissing in the snow

watched

by starlings

Bruce Leeming

a kiss on each cheek
traffic tearing past
in both directions

David Cobb

at the quick-serve till
checked out with each item
her engagement ring

David Cobb

after the quake
adding I love you
to a letter

MICHAEL DYLAN WELCH

"Will you stop, please?"
when she says it in a *low* voice
I may get lucky

Senryu / *Tr. Makoto Ueda*

Making love—building
card castles till the last card
brings them crashing down

ALVARO MUTIS / TR. JAMES KIRKUP

Pink butterflies
the hands of love
give warmth

Anna Santoro / *Tr. Manu Bazzano*

Summer afternoon:
through bars of light your shoulder
rising and falling.

D. C. Trent

Swinging on the hanger
her white summer dress:
       wind chimes

George Swede

naked you sit
in a wicker chair
kneeling
I'm a bird nestfallen

Gabriel Rosenstock

How soft is the nap
  of a female bear's skin
    when a male's is near.

SEISHI YAMAGUCHI /
TR. TAKASHI KODAIRA AND ALFRED H. MARKS

Late August
I bring him the garden
in my skirt.

Alexis Rotella

Her body so beautiful
The Old Man resolves to do
something about his own

Steve Sanfield

his bicycle

on hers—path

by the meadow

John O'Connor

Indian summer…
two lovers rolling
on a bed of leaves

Giovanni Malito

parkbench
lovers pantomime
the Kama Sutra

William Hart

lovers' beach walk
they can feel the moisture
after sunset

WERNER REICHHOLD

pressed rose petals—
their nude bodies
on wet sand

Raffael de Gruttola

On the shore
smooth, round boulders—
her hand-cupped breasts

Bruce Leeming

Heat waves—
cats worship
the God of Love.

Issa Kobayashi / Tr. Lucien Stryk

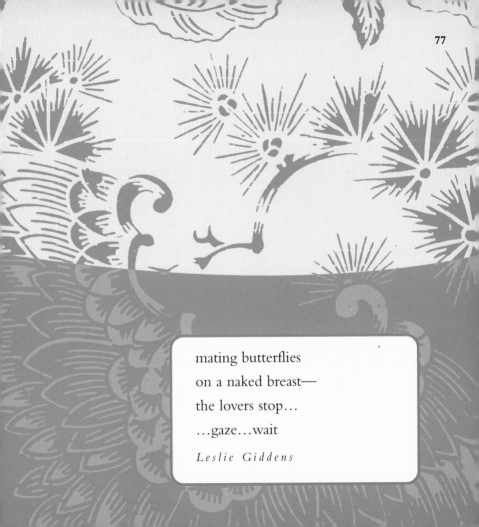

mating butterflies
on a naked breast—
the lovers stop…
…gaze…wait

Leslie Giddens

holding you
in me still…
sparrow songs

ANITA VIRGIL

We curled together,
warm in the softness of leaves,
the winter cradle.

William Alderson

Afternoon tryst.
Undressed, trembling—
watched by a pigeon

Bruce Leeming

Butterfly kidnapped
from butterfly—
all's a-flutter.

Seisensui / Tr. Lucien Stryk

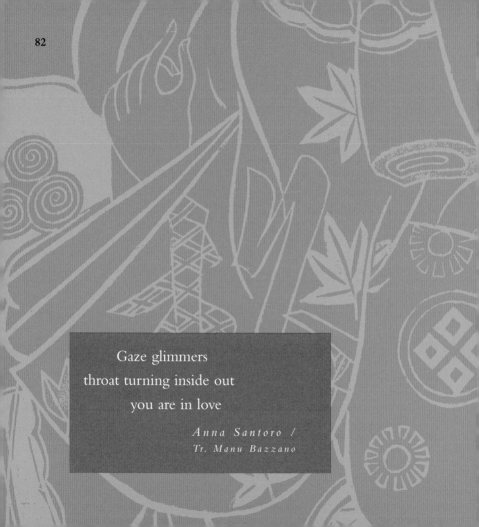

Gaze glimmers
throat turning inside out
you are in love

Anna Santoro /
Tr. Manu Bazzano

"I love you"
such brief words, yet how hard
to say them!

Senryu / Tr. Makoto Ueda

we sweat on our beds
after each climax
the rain never stops

David Cobb

midnight
your thumb strums my nipple
a creak on the stair

Jackie Hardy

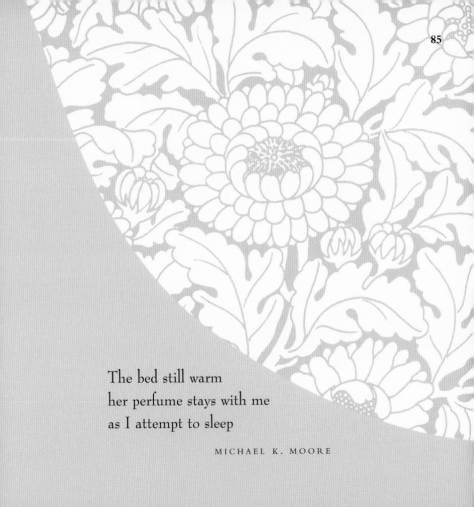

The bed still warm
her perfume stays with me
as I attempt to sleep

MICHAEL K. MOORE

spring love—
the curtains breathe in,
and out

Kevin Bailey

Moonlight caresses
her voluptuousness:
jealous, the stars stare.

Bruce Leeming

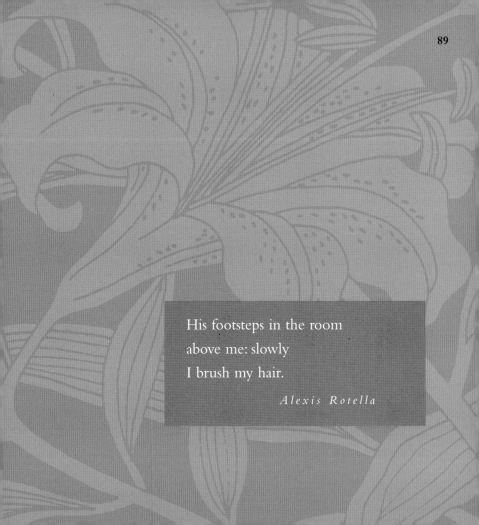

His footsteps in the room
above me: slowly
I brush my hair.

Alexis Rotella

Summer Sunday—
across the breakfast table
brown eyes

Anita Packwood

on my return
she brings blue plums
on a white plate

L. A. Davidson

The first night,
The elopers
Stay at the beautiful place.

Hisui / Tr. R. H. Blyth

how beautiful
she looks—a bride
with nothing on

SENRYU / TR. MAKOTO UEDA

a room with a view—
making love
in the mirror

Philip Rowland

trilliums rippling…
under her scarf
her pulse

Rod Willmot

the small gasp
in the throat of a lover.
No going back.

Giles Goodland

my full red rose—
the weight of it
surprises you

FRANK DULLAGHAN

The lover has a key
to the small gate.

KYORAI / TR. LENORE MAYHEW

the bones of a bird
on the spring path of lovers
not saying a word

Raymond Roseliep

Poverty also,
    In excess,—
And they laugh together.

Kijiro / Tr. R. H. Blyth

Silence, and I watch
The soft cascade of her hair
Shimmer in the dark.

Gilbert Bowen

My tongue on her skin
uncoils desire:
oh, exploring hands!

BRUCE LEEMING

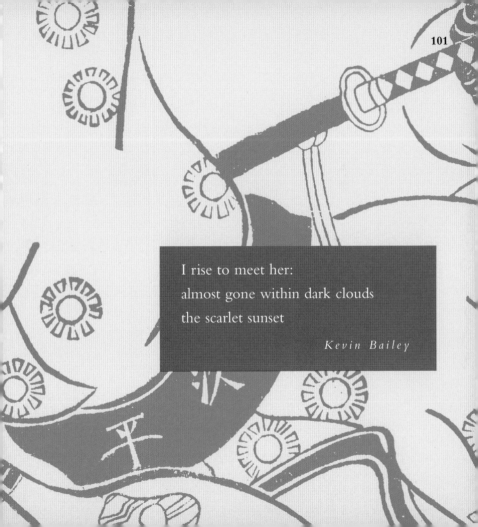

I rise to meet her:
almost gone within dark clouds
the scarlet sunset

Kevin Bailey

In the dust
  on the carriage window:
    I ♥ U

John McDonald

singing a love song
    into her ansaphone

Manu Bazzano

the window pane squeaks
as my finger daubs your name
then mine

ANDREW DETHERIDGE

A haiku is enough
given the complicity
of the girl at the window

John Aspinall

bathing, I think of you
and lift the straw blind
to the rain

ROD WILLMOT

With wine glasses
we stand and talk
into the rhododendrons.

Alexis Rotella

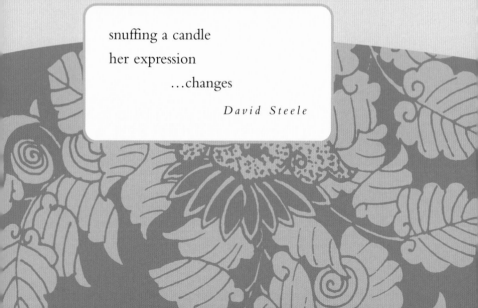

snuffing a candle
her expression
.....changes

David Steele

*Men, women
and their shadows—
dancing*

Santoka / Tr. Fumiko and Akira Yamamoto

2

Bittersweet

STARING AT THE embers of the bonfire after a night of passion, we feel the first shivers of the dawn. The lover's face is no longer so radiant. Could it be an effect of the light?

As the honeymoon fades, we have the opportunity to deepen our union. The end of the honeymoon could be the beginning of a deeper love.

This phase of the journey translates for some into a time of separation. Alongside the pain of breaking up, we find that sweetness and gentle melancholy color our days and nights, giving us fresh insights into our human condition. Some say "a broken heart is an open heart," and that we cannot know true happiness without tasting the bitter wine of disappointment.

If, however, we persevere through the difficulties, we gradually enter a new stage in the journey. We start to understand true intimacy, and learn other facets of ourselves and of the beloved. We get to know our lover's shadow, and aspects of his personality that were hidden to us, perhaps even to him. At this stage, lovers become companions, they take together the first tentative steps in sharing love's journey.

This stage requires courage and humor. We are ready to show a more vulnerable, ordinary side to the other. As peak experiences slowly fade into the plateau of daily life, we need to remind ourselves that we are on a journey, and that new peaks always await us.

hearing us argue,
our old dog tiptoes past
her empty water bowl

Carol Montgomery

if I were a cat
I could sit on your crossword
with my back to you

Jane Whittle

*lone woman singing
to the river while her man
carries on fishing*

Colin Blundell

leaving you
on the crowded train
alone

FRANK DULLAGHAN

after early rain
flowers open to the sun
I miss you

Kate Hall

magnolia leaves
clattering in sudden gusts—
his departure

Linda Jeannette Ward

After we make up
on my ear lobe
black mascara.

SEÁN O'CONNOR

their hands touch
then their feet—in no time
an armistice

Senryu / *Tr. Makoto Ueda*

After drinking and quarreling,
Going back silently,
Under the Milky Way.

Tomoji / *Tr. R. H. Blyth*

by the pleasure boats
our last night—
new moon setting

KEN COCKBURN

尾州名所圖會

辰

津島

天王祭り

Not knowing what to say
he mails
only the envelope

John Brandi

no letter from you
watching a mocking bird
chase a butterfly

Raffael de Gruttola

*After an affair
sweeping
all the rooms.*

Alexis Rotella

doorbell unanswered:
in the porch, my lover's bike
—saddle still warm

CHARLES BRIEN

The tearful parting,
　The porter carrying their things
Busily.

Eishi / Tr. R. H. Blyth

dense fog—

I write your name

on the airport window

Michael Dylan Welch

Airport:
farewell kisses
flying high

Subhaga Failla

For me leaving
for you staying
two autumns

Yosa   Buson   /
Tr. Fumiko and Akira Yamamoto

saying good-bye
snow melting
from the roof tiles

Margaret Chula

Returning in heavy snow
and writing a letter
to my wife

SANTOKA / TR. FUMIKO AND AKIRA YAMAMOTO

The lips you kiss
in a photo
have no warmth.

Subhaga Failla

Drumming rain—she
asleep, warm in passion's wake:
my tears taste of salt.

Bruce Leeming

The arch of her back,
her curved breasts' allure,
haunted all his years.

Bruce Leeming

heated discussion
the ceiling fan
stirs the air

John Crook

My wife holds
a thistle—I feel its prickles
in my hand.

Hino Sojo / *Tr. Makoto Ueda*

breakfast in silence
both halves of the grapefruit
unsweetened

DAVID COBB

my coat dripping
two hours in the rain
without you

FRANK DULLAGHAN

*Suddenly
remembering her,
his feet crushed gravel.*

Kusatao / Tr. Lucien Stryk

In the garbage bin
mound of snow
and a valentine.

Alexis Rotella

He says a word,
and I say a word—autumn
is deepening.

Kyoshi Takahama / Tr. Makoto Ueda

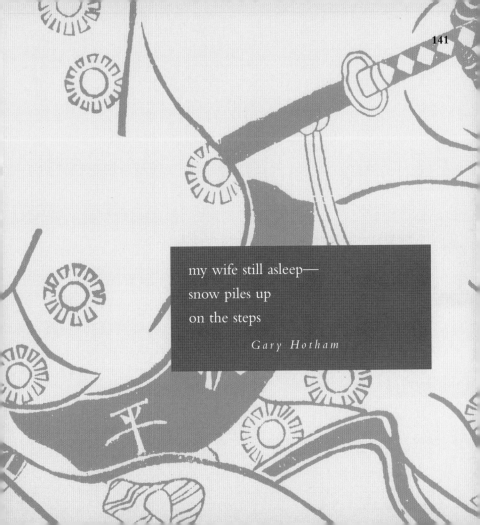

my wife still asleep—
snow piles up
on the steps

Gary Hotham

she has gone—
a vase of wild asters
on the kitchen table

Richard Crist

this night
your answering
machine unplugged

NICK PEARSON

Since you went away
No flowers are left on earth.

Natsume Soseki / Tr. Jonathan Clements

So languidly
snowflakes fall, offering no
consolation to me.

Ishida Hakyo / Tr. Makoto Ueda

His turn to cook
again he can't find
the thyme

CAROLINE G. BANKS

*Sunday morning sex
lasts only as long as the
children's video*

Gerald England

In the waves no trace
remains, though I have swum there
with a woman.

Seishi Yamaguchi / Tr. Makoto Ueda

I close my eyes
and bask in the warmth of love
that is long past.

Hino Sojo / Tr. Makoto Ueda

During our argument
a pink rose
tightens its petals.

ALEXIS ROTELLA

her silence at dinner
sediment
            hanging in the wine

Scott Montgomery

Lightning flashes
where my wife has come from,
whither I go.

Ishida Hakyo / Tr. Makoto Ueda

we should have known it
a November fifth wedding
had to mean fireworks

Phillip Murrell

Making up a quarrel,
    Apparently ashamed
To be the first to smile.

SENRYU / TR. R. H. BLYTH

*On the face
that last night called me names—
morning sunbeam*

George Swede

She sulks,
says nothing, and becomes
a white rose.

Hino Sojo / Tr. Makoto Ueda

Clutching a fist of hair
from my brush
I watch him sleep.

Alexis Rotella

...and another thing
exactly as he left it—
his old pruning hook

Louise Somers Winder

a broken heart
is an open
heart

Anon.

saying nothing—
just the moon rising
a little more

John O'Connor

fallen oak
the initials he carved
girlfriends ago

Steve Dolphy

After
our quarrel,
a full moon

MARGARET SAUNDERS

last goodbye—
his ashes on the water
gold-flecked waves

for Brian
Winona Baker

unexpected news
she stands staring into
the cutlery drawer

Dee Evetts

Sudden shower—
a woman looking out
alone

Otsuyu / Tr. Fumiko and Akira Yamamoto

At the deepest point
    of grief, somebody nearby
        breaks a withered branch.

Seishi Yamaguchi /
Tr. Takashi Kodaira and Alfred H. Marks

she leaves—
　　warm pillow scent
　　remaining

Michael McClintock

in the same room
but not feeling what you feel—
summer breeze

Lee Gurga

3

Harmony

IN MUSIC, two individual notes create a deeper resonance when strung together in "harmony." Of the three hundred or so love songs transmitted by the troubadours, we know only their melodies, but not their tempo. This wasn't the result of neglect, but a deliberate act, known to music lovers as "Tempo Rubato," which allows greater freedom of interpretation of each love song, according to mood, circumstances, and temperament. Seized by love, we might want to speed up, pause, or slow the tempo right down.

Love, unlike religion or politics, is hard to canonize. There are as many ways to reach the peak of love's journey as there are people. The common element is a certain quality of merging, of slow dissolution of the individual self.

Here, the journey through the wilderness and the arid desert, through the hurdles of time and the hostilities of territory, reaches its goal, its final station ("ecstase" in greek)—the merging into the other and the disappearance of the self. This is also the goal of spiritual practice and of Zen in particular, which is the very bone and marrow of all good haiku. From the standpoint of harmonic love, death itself is a fiction, and romantic love only the ABC, the net of seduction stealing us into the possibility of a more spacious life.

The way in which such merging happens while the two lovers maintain their individuality is what some good love haiku point at, with their characteristic humor and warmth.

the pages flutter softly
through three chapters,
while you sleep

Andrew Detheridge

Watching you get up,
I slide into the warm space
that you leave behind.

Andrew Shimield

sharing a sandwich:
my mouth   your mouth

Ross Clark

longing to be near her
i remember my shirt
hanging in her closet

NICK AVIS

My beloved's arm,
    above the sparkler she holds,
       shining in the gloom.

Seishi Yamaguchi /
Tr. Takashi Kodaira and Alfred H. Marks

The telephone poles,
    so ugly on the landscape,
        bring your lovely voice.

Dorothy Cameron Smith

*I set the alarm
get out of bed to unpack
her photograph*

Dee Evetts

it nullifies
all the treatments by the doctor—
his wife's beauty

Senryu / Tr. *Makoto Ueda*

against the cold,
we lie together like spoons,
old friends in old skin

MICHAEL FACHERTY

Still playing with words—
an old couple linked
by a lifetime of scrabble

Noragh Jones

My wife—blurred
in my right eye,
*   clear in my left.*

Hino Sojo / Tr. Lucien Stryk

the whole bed
yet he lays his head
in my hand

Jane Reichhold

As day breaks...
    the lightness of her breath
        on my back

TOM TICO

The rainy season;
I gaze out at the rain,
    My wife standing behind me.

Rinka / Tr. R. H. Blyth

puddle after puddle—
the bright color
of her long raincoat

Gary Hotham

spellbound husband
his wife's version
of their courtship

Francine Porad

Methodical husband:
On his list of chores, she finds
Her name

Anita Krumins

They are going out together;
The husband
Speaks to the mirror.

Seiko / Tr. R. H. Blyth

birth mark
on her cheek—a rain cloud
at nightfall

John O'Connor

I touch your left breast,
a soft white pouch in my hand,
holding everything.

NEIL HOPKINS

*her back freckled
like a field
of brown poppies*

Kevin Bailey

Valentine's Day—
she reminds me
to fasten my seatbelt

Michael Dylan Welch

French waitress
my wife refocuses
my attention

John Crook

The wind in the pines
makes me lonely for you
a mile from home

JAMES NORTON

homecoming:
a two-day growth of beard
bristles her nipple…

David Cobb

Against his coat
I brush my lips—
the silence of snowflakes.

Alexis Rotella

We laugh and kiss
picking strange pebbles
by a roaring sea

KEN JONES

between my hands
the moon
on your face

Frank Dullaghan

The autumn tempest:
Looking at one another
In the candle-light.

Sekito / Tr. R. H. Blyth

*Moon
and melon cooling
with us in the stream*

Peggy Willis Lyles

in your room
still warm...
the sleeveless dress

Brian David Johnston

hottest night
naked on the bed
apart   together

DAVID STEELE

tonight
two crickets
are singing

Toshimi Horiuchi

The end of summer,
but Love-in-a-Mist
starts to flower again.

Patricia V. Dawson

green fields:
two white butterflies
become one

Toshimi Horiuchi

His first letters:
at each cleanup again
they survive.

Wanda Reumer

wallpaper flowers
have not faded
behind your photo

David Walker

you stand
framed in my window
moonlight through the trees

JACKIE HARDY

Waiting by her,
     As she ties her sash,
Holding his chin.

Nakibo / Tr. R. H. Blyth

night comes—
picking up your shoes
still warm

Gary Hotham

sleepless—
hoping you'll wake
so we can argue

Daniel Trent

so large at dusk
they argue whether
it is Venus

JANICE BOSTOK

Sunrise:
I forget my side
of the argument

George Swede

A sigh from her
then one from me—
two pages turn

George Swede

your breathing
moves my book——wind rises
in the trees

Jane Whittle

Don't weep, insects—
lovers, stars themselves,
must part.

Issa Kobayashi / *Tr. Lucien Stryk*

in the mirrors on her dress
little pieces of my
self

Cor van den Heuvel

Among the graffiti
The name of
Beloved you.

Matsuo Basho / Tr. Alex Kerr

night of no moon
I turn on every light
to read your letter

Marco Fraticelli

solar eclipse

and at the darkest point

you call my name

Claire Bugler Hewitt

Only I laugh
at his joke...
the silence.

Alexis Rotella

*chill night
after you the toilet seat
slightly warm*

Dee Evetts

Wife in a good mood
I don't tell her about
the snake in the grass

George Swede

fresh from the bath
she leans—two drops of water
catch the light

David Steele

daybreak—
    working as one,
        two butterflies.

ISSA KOBAYASHI / TR. LUCIEN STRYK

undressing for love:
the click of our spectacles
folded together

                    Brian Tasker

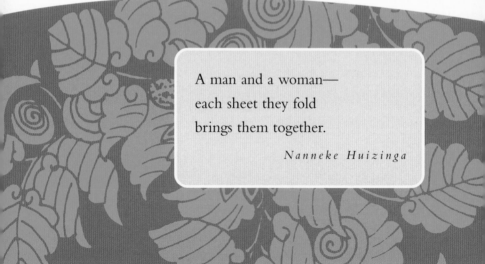

A man and a woman—
each sheet they fold
brings them together.

Nanneke Huizinga

first snow
lites our bedroom
she puts on the flowered sheets

LeRoy Gorman

warm wine
the sharing of thoughts
a widening sky

Joanna Ashwell

last bale of hay—
we sit down on it
and watch the moon

LEE GURGA

this summer night—
she lets the firefly glow
through the cage of her fingers

Gary Hotham

old married couple
crossing the bridge at twilight
wear similar coats

Adrian Keefe

*Imagined: sitting
with old woman, both in tears,
gazing at the moon.*

Matsuo Basho / Tr. Nobuyuki Yuasa

woods walking
            in a time of trilliums
my hand in her hand

anne mckay

Lifting our coffee cups
simultaneously
This must be the plateau

Adrian Keefe

snow now rain—
your picture
by mine

GARY HOTHAM

the engaged couple:
they catch the same cold, one
after the other

Senryu / Tr. Makoto Ueda

at the airport
our unspent coins—
sights we didn't see

KEN COCKBURN

time to go—
the stones we threw
at the bottom of the ocean

Gary Hotham

going on holiday
we show each other
our special clothes

FRED SCHOFIELD

*Whatever she wears
she becomes beautiful—
moon-viewing*

Chiyo / Tr. Fumiko and Akira Yamamoto

Slowly they grew apart.
Fifty years on   their gravestones
lean together

Edward D. Glover

A man and his wife
Are pushing the hand-cart,
  Saying something to each other.

Itto / Tr. R. H. Blyth

On our evening walk
a tree with no name
blooming

Manu Bazzano

Sitting silently
in our bedroom
April shower

Manu Bazzano

The two lovers
bow together
to the medicine Buddha.*

Manu Bazzano

(*) Offerings and prostrations to the medicine Buddha can be of great help in time of crisis and illness. A deity in the Buddhist pantheon, the medicine Buddha also represents the innate qualities for healing present in human beings.

a smell of jasmine tea
drifting after love
rainy cottage

Ikuyo Yoshimura

While we wait
to do it again,
the rains of spring

Michael McClintock

I have known lovers...
Cherry-bloom...the nightingale...
I will sleep content

Anon. / Tr. Peter Beilenson

The morning cold:
smelling of tooth powder,
my wife's mouth.

Hino Sojo / Tr. Makoto Ueda

The fiddler's wife
watching his fingers move
knits him a scarf

KIM PAUL RICHARDSON

sunset kiss—
our faces turning
slowly orange

Kevin Bailey

Let's take
the duckweed way
to clouds.

Issa Kobayashi /
Tr. Lucien Stryk

winter moon
nudge of the unborn child
between us

Jean Jorgensen

waves pound the shore
   you turn
   in your sleep

Caroline Gourlay

Hazy moonlight night:
there must be love for
unlikely faces too.

Natsume Soseki / Tr. Makoto Ueda

*Love.
So many different ways
to have been in love.*

Boncho / Tr. Lenore Mayhew

The moment two bubbles
are united, they both vanish.
A lotus blooms.

MURAKAMI KIJO / TR. MAKOTO UEDA

Acknowledgments

Note: Every effort has been made to contact copyright holders; the editor would be pleased to hear from any copyright holders not acknowledged below.

William Alderson: "We curled" from *HQ Poetry Magazine* 11/12. **Anon:** "I have known" tr. Peter Beilenson from his *A Haiku Garland*. Copyright © 1968 Peter Pauper Press. Used with permission. **Joanna Ashwell:** "placing" from *Blithe Spirit* 11/1, Mar. 2001; "warm wine" from *Blithe Spirit* 11/4, Dec. 2001. Used with permission. **John Aspinall:** "A haiku" from *HQ Poetry Magazine* 5, Winter 1991. **Nick Avis:** "longing" from *The Haiku Anthology* ed. Cor van den Heuvel (W. W. Norton & Co., 1999). Used with permission. **Kevin Bailey:** "spring love," "I rise," "her back," and "sunset." Used with permission. **Winona Baker:** "last goodbye" from her *Even a Stone Breathes* (Oolichan Books, 2000). Used with permission. **Claudia Baldini:** "You kissed" tr. Manu Bazzano from the original in *Luna a Mezzogiorno* compiled by Rosetta Berardi (Edizioni del Girasole, 1998). Used with permission. **Caroline G. Banks:** "His turn" from her *Warm Under the Cat: Haiku and Senryu Poems* (Wellington Press, 1995). **John Barlow:** "early morning" from *The Haiku Anthology* ed. Cor van den Heuvel (W. W. Norton & Co., 1999). Used with permission. **Matsuo Basho:** "Among" tr. Alex Kerr from *Lost Japan* (Lonely Planet, 1996); "Imagined" from *Full Moon Rising* (Branden Books, 1976). Permission courtesy of Branden Books. **Manu Bazzano:** "Lying," "Looking," "Singing," "On our evening walk," "Sitting," and "The two lovers." Used with permission. **Colin Blundell:** "we talked" from *Blithe Spirit* 2/1, Jan. 1992; "lone woman" from *Blithe Spirit* 5/4, November 1995. Used with permission. **Mykel Board:** "Through binoculars" from *The Haiku Anthology* ed. Cor van den Heuvel (W. W. Norton & Co., 1999). Used with permission. **Boncho:** "Love" tr. Leonore Mayhew from her *Monkey's Raincoat* (Charles E. Tuttle and Co., 1985). Used with permission. **Janice Bostok:** "so large" from *Blithe Spirit* 6/1, Feb. 1996. Used with permission. **Gilbert Bowen:** "She is naked" from *HQ Poetry Magazine* 6, Spring 1992; "Silence" from *HQ Poetry Magazine* 1, Winter 1990. **John Brandi:** "Not knowing" from his *Weeding the Cosmos* (La Alameda Press, 1994). Copyright © 1994 John Brandi. Used with permission. **Charles Brien:** "doorbell" from *Blithe Spirit* 5/3, Aug. 1995. Used with permission. **Yosa Buson:** "Makes the eye happy" tr. Robert Hass from *The Essential Haiku* ed/intro. Robert Hass (The Ecco Press, 1994). Copyright © 1994 Robert Hass. Reprinted by permission of HarperCollins, Inc.; "For me" tr. Fumiko and Akira Yamamoto from *Haiku People Big and Small* ed. Stephen Addiss (Weatherhill, 1998). Used with permission. **Chiyo:** "Whatever she wears" tr. Fumiko and Akira Yamamoto from *Haiku People Big and Small* ed. Stephen Addiss (Weatherhill, 1998). Used with permission. **Kaga no Chiyo:** "moon flowers!" tr. Patricia Donegan and Yoshie Ishibashi from *Chiyo-ni: Woman*

ed. William J. Higginson (Kodansha International, 1996). Used with permission. **Kusatao:** "Suddenly" tr. Lucien Stryk from his *Cage of Fireflies* (Swallow Press/Ohio University Press, 1993). Translation copyright © 1993 Lucien Stryk. Reprinted with permission of Swallow Press/Ohio University Press. **Kyorai:** "The lover" tr. Leonore Mayhew from her *Monkey's Raincoat* (Charles E. Tuttle and Co., of Boston, Massachusetts and Tokyo, Japan, 1985). Used with permission. **Takahama Kyoshi:** "He says a word" tr. Makoto Ueda from his *Modern Japanese Haiku* (University of Toronto Press, 1976). Translation copyright © 1976 Makoto Ueda. Reprinted with permission of the publisher. **Bruce Leeming:** "Kissing" from *Blithe Spirit* 11/1, Mar. 2001; "On the shore" and "Afternoon tryst" from his *Engraving the Sky* (Richard Joseph, 1993). Copyright © 1993 Bruce Leeming; "Moonlight caresses," "My tongue," "Drumming rain," and "The arch of her back" from his *Poems in the Haiku Manner* (1991). Copyright © 1991 Bruce Leeming. Used with permission. **Peggy Willis Lyles:** "Moon" from her *To Hear the Rain* (Brooks Books, 2002). Copyright © 2002 Peggy Lyles. Used with permission. **Giovanni Malito:** "Indian summer…" from *Blithe Spirit* 11/4, Dec. 2001. Used with permission. **Michael McClintock:** "she leaves," and "while we wait" from his *Maya* (Seer Ox Press, 1975). Copyright © 1975 Michael McClintock. Used with permission. **John McDonald:** "In the dust" from *Blithe Spirit* 11/4, Dec. 2001. Used with permission. **anne mckay:** "woods walking" from her *the journey* (2001). Used with permission. **Carol Montgomery:** "hearing us argue" from *The Haiku Anthology* ed. Cor van den Heuvel (W. W. Norton & Co., 1999). **Scott Montgomery:** "her silence" from *The Haiku Anthology* ed. Cor van den Heuvel (W. W. Norton & Co., 1999). **Michael K. Moore:** "The bed" from *Blithe Spirit* 10/4, Dec. 2000. Used with permission. **Phillip Murrell:** "we should have known it" from *Blithe Spirit* 11/4, Dec. 2001. Used with permission. **Alvaro Mutis:** "Making love" tr. James Kirkup from *Blithe Spirit* 2/4, Oct. 1992. **Nakibo:** "Waiting" tr. R. H. Blyth from his *Senryu* (Greenwood Press, 1971). **James Norton:** "The wind" from *Blithe Spirit* 5/1, Feb.1995. Used with permission. **John O'Connor:** "his bicycle" first published in *Sky Falling* (NZ); "birth mark" first published in *Spin* (NZ); "saying nothing" formerly unpublished. Used with permission. **Seán O'Connor:** "Watched her approach," and "After we make up" from *Pilgrim Foxes* (Pilgrim Press, 2001). Used with permission. **Otsuyo:** "Sudden shower" tr. Fumiko and Akira Yamamoto from *Haiku People Big and Small* ed. Stephen Addiss (Weatherhill, 1998). **Anita Packwood:** "Summer Sunday" from *Blithe Spirit* 5/4, November 1995. **Nick Pearson:** "this night" from *HQ Poetry Magazine* 23/24. Used with permission. **Francine Porad:** "spellbound" from *Haiku Zasshi Zo*, Summer/Fall 1988. Used with permission. **Jane Reichhold:** "the whole bed" from *Blithe Spirit* 2/4, Oct. 1992. Used with permission. **Werner Reichhold:** "lovers" from *HQ Poetry Magazine* 2, Spring 1991. Used with permission. **Wanda Reumer:** "His first letters" from *Haiku World* ed. William J. Higginson (Kodansha International, 1996). **Kim Paul Richardson:** "The fiddler's wife" from *Blithe Spirit* 10/4, Dec. 2000. **Rinka:** "The rainy season" tr. R. H. Blyth from his *A History of Haiku* (The Hokuseido Press, 1964). Copyright © 1964 R. H. Blyth. **Raymond Roseliep:** "the bones" from

with permission of the publisher. **David Steele:** "he looks again" from *HQ Poetry Magazine* 25; "snuffing a candle" formerly unpublished; "hottest night" from *Blithe Spirit*, Sept. 1998; "fresh" from *The Acorn Book of Contemporary Haiku* ed. Lucien Stryk and Kevin Bailey (Acorn Book Co., 2000). Used with permission. **John Stevenson:** "too quick" from *The Haiku Anthology* ed. Cor van den Heuvel (W. W. Norton and Co., 1999). **George Swede:** "Swinging," "On the face," "Sunrise," and "A sigh" from *The Haiku Anthology* ed. Cor van den Heuvel (W. W. Norton & Co., 1999); "Wife" from *HQ Poetry Magazine* 6, Spring 1992; "She removes" from *HQ Poetry Magazine* 9. Used with permission. **Takeo:** "I will share" tr. R. H. Blyth from his *A History of Haiku* (The Hokuseido Press, 1964). Copyright © 1964 R. H. Blyth. **Brian Tasker:** "all my expectations" from *HQ Poetry Magazine* 7/8, Summer and Fall 1992; "morning shyness" from his *the sound of rain* (the Bare Bones press, 1999). Copyright © 1999 Brian Tasker; "after she's gone" and "undressing" from his *a ragbag of haiku* (the Bare Bones press, 1999). Copyright © 1999 Brian Tasker. Used with permission. **Maurice Tasnier:** "her second look…" from *Blithe Spirit* 11/4, Dec. 2001; "kept awake" from *Time Haiku* ed. Erica Facey (Eleven, 2000). Used with permission. **Tom Tico:** "As day breaks" from *Spring Morning Sun* (San Francisco, 1998). Used with permission. **Tomoji:** "After drinking" tr. R. H. Blyth from his *A History of Haiku* (The Hokuseido Press, 1964). Copyright © 1964 R. H. Blyth. **D. C. Trent:** "Summer afternoon" from *Haiku World* ed. William J. Higginson (Kodansha International, 1996). **Daniel Trent:** "sleepless" from *Blithe Spirit* 5/4, Nov. 1995. **Cor van den Heuvel:** "in the mirrors." Copyright © 1999 Cor van den Heuvel. Used with permission. **Anita Virgil:** "holding you" from *The Haiku Anthology* ed. Cor van den Heuvel (W. W. Norton & Co., 1999). Used with permission. **David Walker:** "wallpaper" from *HQ Poetry Magazine* 25. Used with permission. **Linda Jeannette Ward:** "magnolia leaves" from *Blithe Spirit* 10/2, June 2000. Used with permission. **Michael Dylan Welch:** "after the quake" from *Mirrors* 3/1, Winter 1990; "dense fog" from *Frogpond* 20/3, Dec. 1997; "Valentine's Day" from *Frogpond* 24/1, Spring 2001. Used with permission. **Maggie West:** "tissue paper" from *Blithe Spirit* 7/2, May 1997. Used with permission. **Jane Whittle:** "if" from *Blithe Spirit* 9/4, Dec. 1999. Copyright © 1999 Jane Whittle; "your breathing" from *Blithe Spirit* 11/4, Dec. 2001. Used with permission. **Rod Willmot:** "away from eyes," "trilliums," and "bathing" from *The Haiku Anthology* ed. Cor van den Heuvel (W. W. Norton & Co., 1999). **Louise Somers Winder:** "…and another thing" from *The Anthology of Western World Haiku Society 1980 Haiku Award Winners* compiled by Lorraine Ellis Harr. Copyright © 1981 Lorraine Ellis Harr. **Nick Woodward:** "failing to intrude" from *Blithe Spirit* 11/4, Dec. 2001. **Seishi Yamaguchi:** "Festival pathos," "The lily," "Peach trees," "The shrine maiden," "How soft," "At the deepest point," and "My beloved" tr. Takashi Kodaira and Alfred H. Marks from *The Essence of Modern Haiku* (Mangajin, Inc., 1993); "In the waves" tr. Makoto Ueda from his *Modern Japanese Haiku* (University of Toronto Press, 1976). Translation copyright © 1976 Makoto Ueda. Reprinted with permission of the publisher. **Ikuyo Yoshimura:** "a smell" from his *Spring Thunder* (Rainbow Press, 1996). Copyright © 1996 Ikuyo Yoshimura. Used with permission.

Picture Credits

16 Lovers from the "Poem of the Pillow," ("Uta makura"), by Kitagawa Utamaro. Victoria & Albert Museum, London/Bridgeman Art Library **32** Swallows and Peach Blossom in Moonlight by Ando or Utagawa Hiroshige. Leeds Museums and Galleries (City art Gallery)/Bridgeman Art Library **40** Six-Fold Screen Depicting Reeds and Cranes by Suzuki Kiitsu. The Detroit Institute of Arts/Bridgeman Art Library **49** A "Shunga" (erotic) print: Lovers Listening to a Cuckoo by Ippitsusai Buncho. Private Collection/Bridgeman Art Library **57** Shin Bijin (True Beauties) depicting a woman with a fan by Toyohara Chikanobu. Oriental Museum, Durham University/Bridgeman Art Library **64** Courtesan and Lover by Sigimura Jihei. Art Institute of Chicago/Bridgeman Art Library **73** Lovers from the "Poem of the Pillow," ("Uta makura"), by Kitagawa Utamaro. British Library, London/Bridgeman Art Library **81** Chrysanthemums. Chester Beatty Library, London/Bridgeman Art Library **88** Suminoto of Okanaya by Isoda Koryusai. British Federation of Master Printers/Bridgeman Art Library **110** Godamme. Act V from the "Chushingura Series" by Kitagawa Utamaro. Arts Council Collection, Hayward Gallery, London/Bridgeman Art Library **121** Decorated Boats at the Sanno Festival at Tsushima, Owari Province by Ando or Utagawa Hiroshige. Blackburn Museum and Art Gallery, Lancashire/Bridgeman Art Library **128** Maples at Mama by Ando or Utagawa Hiroshige. British Library, London/Bridgeman Art Library **145** Snow Scene in the Garden of a Daimyo by Ando or Utagawa Hiroshige. Leeds Museums and Galleries (Lotherton Hall/Bridgeman Art Library **152** Fireworks, Riogoku by Ando or Utagawa Hiroshige. Fitzwilliam Museum, University of Cambridge/Bridgeman Art Library **161** View from Satta Suruga Province by Ando or Utagawa Hiroshige. Ashmolean Museum, Oxford/Bridgeman Art Library **166** The Lovers Hambei and O'chie by Kitagawa Utamaro. British Library, London/Bridgeman Art Library **185** Girl with a mirror by Kitagawa Utamaro. British Library, London/Bridgeman Art Library **192** Improving weather at Enoshima by Utagawa Kunisada. Victoria & Albert Museum, London/Bridgeman Art Library **208** Flowers and Insects by Maekawa Bunrei. British Library, London/Bridgeman Art Library **217** Girl washing linen by Shinsui. British Library, London/Bridgeman Art Library **224** Autumn maple leaves on the Tsutaya River by Katsushika Hokusai. British Museum, London/Bridgeman Art Library **240** One of a series of paintings of birds and fruit by Wang Guochen. School of Oriental & African Studies Library, University of London/Bridgeman Art Library **249** Heron and lotus by Yamamoto Baiitsu. Private Collection/Bridgeman Art Library